I0494014

China
hijacks
Karl Marx

Modayil George

i

Copyright © 2012 Modayil George

All rights reserved.

ISBN:1499178476
ISBN-13:9781499178470

ii

DEDICATION

Dedicated to my family.

CONTENTS

ACKNOWLEDGMENTS

The book is produced with the information available on the internet.

The information available on the internet on the Australian Laws has been very useful.

In addition, the information provided by Landgate Perth, State Administrative Tribunal Perth & Federal Court of Australia is acknowledged.

Foreword

This is a book of facts. All information provided are well corroborated & can be verified.

Some parts of the information provided are the logical conclusions of the author from the data provided here. The readers can grasp the logic as script explains the logic.

No personal prejudice is intended.

The information on iron ore data is available on the internet from IMF, USGS etc.

The purpose of the book is to urge the world to regulate cheating in trade as it is the main source of financial imbalances widening the gap between the poor & the rich.

In particular, undue profit making in trade is the most serious issue which causes inequality among us.

The world is ignoring this crime while preoccupying with minor crimes.

It is important for the world to appreciate that making undue profit in trade particularly in essential consumer goods is a serious crime.

It is for the world to prohibit such conduct by publicity, by persuasion, by legislation & by agreements.

Modayil George

1:   The Wheatgate

Greenspan bribes Saddam Hussein

In year 2001, United Nation's sanctions against Saddam Hussein's regime in Iraq were in place.

At that time, top spies of CIA visited Saddam Hussein's brother –in-law secretly & against the provisions of UN sanctions to make some secret deals under the secret instructions of Donald Rumsfeld. Finally this resulted in lucrative wheat exports to Iraq & a payment of bribes to Saddam's cronies totaling $221.67 million by the American Wheat Board. The payment of the bribes totaling $221.67 million was paid by bank notes secretly printed by the Treasury & with the knowledge of Alan Greenspan.

When a senate enquiry found these facts, President George Bush distanced himself from all these matters and said of Alan Greenspan as follows: "It has not crossed my mind that he would have behaved badly".

If we did not hear of this incredible story, it is because it did not happen in USA but it happened in Australia.

And the real players were the Australian counter parts. The words were of Premier John Howard spoken of Australian Wheat Board (AWB) on 13 April, 2006.

These matters are recorded by UN investigator Paul Volker.

It is on record that AWB or Australian Wheat Board paid the said amount of bribe to Iraq.

It is also on record that National Printing Agency (NPA) working under the instructions of Reserve Bank of Australia printed the notes in secrecy which were used to bribe & secure wheat deals for AWB.

After exporting record amount of wheat to Iraq under humanitarian grounds during the Iraq war, AWB folded after the wheat scandal in 2006.

The ongoing reporting by Australian newspapers indicates that current Reserve Bank Governor Glenn Stevens may have ordered the deals under the secret instruction from Peter Costello, the then Finance Minister of Australia.

John Howard's words indicate that he may have known the deals in advance.

We should wonder why some government officials in Australian Wheat Board should engage in such organized conduct if the orders did not come from Howard, Costello & Glenn Stephens.

Can such things happen without their knowledge?

Who is coordinating such elaborate secret deals within Australian Wheat Board, National Printing Agency & Reserve Bank of Australia?

What we learn from these matters as a minimum is that Reserve Bank of Australia is playing market games at the behest of the Australian Government.

Government of Australia is capable to bribe Saddam and fight Saddam simultaneously.

Given the gravity of this story, we should not doubt that anything is possible down under in Australia.

How did Australia become an "Instant Billionaire" by 2006 after being only a millionaire in 2000?

Is it a true success story or is it another wheat deal?

2:   *Thai Rice farmers' 15 % profit*

A Vietnamese woman sells rice at her stall in Hanoi. The US Agriculture
Department forecasts Vietnam's rice exports will rise to 7.8 million tonnes this year. EPA

COMPARISON AMONG THREE COUNTRIES IN 2012

	Thailand	Vietnam	Myanmar
Cost (baht/tonne)	9,763	4,070	7,121
Productivity (kg/rai)	450	900	420
Revenue (baht/tonne)	11,319	7,251	10,605
Profit (baht/tonne)	1,555	3,180	3,484

Source: UTT Center for International Trade Studies   POSTgraphics

(Bangkok Post article dated 26 February, 2014)

3: *Rio Tinto's 500% profit*

While rice farmers in Thailand made 15 % profit tilling the soil, Sam Walsh, the chairman of Rio Tinto based in Australia, boasted on 13 March, 2014 as quoted in The Australian that Rio Tinto's cash cost for iron ore production was one of the lowest.

He claimed it was only US $20.70 a tonne for Rio Tinto.

All Rio does is to dig up the God given soil & sell it to the Chinese.

On that day, the iron ore, the dug up soil, was trading in "Shanghai iron ore spot market" at $108 a tonne, a fall from $137 a tonne from April, 2013 & a fall from the all time peak $187 from Feb, 2011.

So while Sam was making 500% on the soil business, the poor Thai rice farmers have to till the same soil, though much softer, to make a mere 15 % gain after a hard days' work.

Why is such a disparity?

If cash cost to dig up the iron ore, God's soil, in Australia is only $20.70, the cash cost for the China to dig it up in China must be much less.

And China is producing more than 50 % of the world's demand in iron ore.

So logically China should not be buying iron ore for anything more than $20 to $30 a tonne.

If we can grow rice for $1 a kilogram, would we buy it at $10 a kilogram even if we are a bit short of it?

There are only five players in this great game of supply and demand and the game of sand & soil at "Shanghai iron ore spot market".

China is the sole buyer of iron ore in Shanghai market

China who makes the sickle and sells them to the poor Thai farmers is the main player & the only buyer.

Then we have the giant Vale from Brazil.

But we have three Australian giants; Sam Wash's Rio Tinto, Jac Nasser's BHP & Andrew Forrest's Fortescue.

So there are four sellers and one buyer in the great "Shanghai iron ore spot market"

It is important for us to determine why China is willing to pay $108 for a tonne of iron ore when they can produce it themselves at a cost of $5 to $10 a tonne.

In 2013, three eminent scholars got a Nobel prize each for economics because of their innovative work in supply and demand.

They were dealing with stock markets, the world casino.

It is quite a subject to figure out how supply and demand may work in a casino. They & their brilliance did not solve the Thai famers' plight.

It is quite likely that their research & theory supported the iron ore market play by Sam Walsh and his friends.

But that makes no sense to ordinary people who are affected by the conduct; how Australians can sell iron ore at $108 a tonne in the name of "global demand" when it can be produced at a cost of less than $20 a tonne.

It was the exclusive advantage of cost of production that propelled China to become the factory of the world.

Does China have a secret desire to inflate the cost of production of iron ore and other raw materials having become the factory of the world by 2000?

Billions of us use sickles and cars made of steel.

Steel is made out of iron ore.

Billions of us are paying for God's soil in one form or other.

So we should use our pea brain and see what is going on in Shanghai in China, in Pilbarra in West Australia & in Thai rice fields.

4: China's X Factor

All Rio Tinto does in the iron ore business is to dig up the God given soil & sell it to the Chinese.

Early in year 2014, the iron ore, the dug up soil, was trading in "Shanghai spot market" at $108 a tonne, a fall from $154 a tonne from February, 2012 & a fall from the peak of $187 a tonne in February, 2011.

It is not the fall that raises the eyebrows. It is the dramatic rise earlier that raises the eyebrows.

Iron Ore price rose to the peak of $187 a tonne in February 2011 from a low of $12.45 a tonne in 2000-2001

The iron ore price had remained fairly stable from 1984 to 2004 within the range between $10 a tonne & $16 a tonne as per IMF data.

We can estimate the cost of iron ore production from this. It ought to be much less than $10 a tonne.

So while Sam is making 500% profit on the soil business, the poor Thai rice farmer has to sweat & toil with the same soil, though much softer, to make mere 15% gain after a hard days' work.

Why is such a disparity? Hard working rice farmers have to contend with 15% profit while high flying Sam enjoys 500% profit.

Why is the market price for iron ore, the dug up soil $108 a tonne, when Sam can dig it up for a cash cost of only $20.70.

Is that market price based on the famous supply & demand theory?

If cash cost to dig up the iron ore, God's soil, in Australia is only $20.70 , the cost for Chinese to dig it up in China must be much less.

They do have plenty iron ore in China. They were the largest iron ore producers since 2004.

Is it truly the so called supply & demand that drives the iron ore price?

We should not of course forget crude oil & other commodities. They are also part of the same game of supply & demand.

But when we try to figure out the dynamics, we should not forget an important aspect form our pea brain.

The iron ore trading price remained within a range of $10 a tonne to $15 a tonne for sixteen long years from 1884 to 2000.

In fact it remained below $16 a tonne until December 2004.

Then in January, 2005 it started trading at a different price level altogether; a jump from $16 a tonne to $28 a tonne.

That is a 75% jump in price almost overnight.

We did not hear that Vale or Rio or BHP was making any loss when they were selling iron ore at $16 and less for over twenty years from 1984 to 2004.

So it is no brainer to figure out that the cost of digging up iron ore was much less than $10 a tonne around the world from 1984 till 2004.

So Rio's cash cost of $20.70 in 2014 should include the cost of Sam's trips to Shanghai.

Let us not forget his expenses in Shanghai. And let us not forget the cost of negotiations with the hard bargainers in Shanghai.

Let us also not forget that diggers' pay around the world did not jump anything abnormal in any period between 1984 until today.

That will bring us to an important question. Does cost of production have anything to do with market prices set by supply & demand?

It is also a no brainer question.

The price of Thai rice does depend on cost of production.

Price of Rolex watches does not depend on the cost of production.

There is an X factor in Rolex prices.

Does iron ore price have any X factor?

5:   The monopoly

Most of the business minded people do business by instinct rather than by calculations. They know most of what is written here by instinct while we laymen have to analyze them.

If you are a good & honest business man, you calculate the cost of your wares & add a profit of 10-30% to arrive at the selling prices.

That is what the rice farmer does. He calculates his total cost of producing the rice as $1 a kg. Then he sells it at $1.15 a kg or more as the market allows him. Most likely he may have forgotten to add the cost of depreciation of his land. The cost of depreciation and cost of finance come from the profit he makes.

Most probably he inherited the land. So his cost of land is almost nothing in his mind.

If his cost was $100 a kg instead of $1 a kg, he would have sold the rice at $115 a kg.

In this case he makes a profit of $15 a kg of rice.

So his effort would have been the same to make $0.15 profit or $15 profit if his cost was $100 a kg instead of $1.00 a kg.

Let us assume that these are true market prices.

So he makes $15 profit if his cost of production was $100.

But he makes only $0.15 profit if his cost of production was only $1.00 for the same product.

That is a strange conclusion. One makes more profit if his cost of production was more rather than less.

But we should not allow ourselves to be confused on this simple matter.

If his cost of production was only $90 a kg, he would have made a profit of $25 a kg as $115 a kg was the true market price.

Or he could sell his rice at only $105 a kg bringing or forcing the market price to come down.

So we are talking here more about global cost of production.

If global cost production was higher for a product, then the producer or manufacturer makes more profit in terms of dollar or cash.

For a farmer, making a cash profit of $15 a kg is more valuable than making $0.15 profit for the same one kg of rice.

Most of the people also know this for a fact. It is a no brainer issue.

By year 2000, China had established itself as the factory of the world.

It established that status because China could make the best Nike shoe at the lowest cost of production globally.

But now , by year 2000 China has driven most competitors out of business.

Soon beyond year 2000, China is dictating the prices of goods in the world.

So if you were producing steel products like valves or pipes, China prefers a much higher iron ore price rather than a lower iron ore price.

In other words, by year 2004, China prefers iron ore to be sold at $187 a tonne rather than at $10 a tonne.

We can simplify this.

By 2004, there was only one factory. It is called China.

By 2004, China had the monopoly of world products particularly of those products made of steel.

Steel is made of iron ore.

By year 2004, the higher the global commodity prices, the better for China.

The world at large would have falsely believed that opposite was true; that China preferred lower commodity prices at any given time & therefore they were bargaining hard with the Australians to bring the commodity prices down on behalf of the billions of people.

The world tiger called Asian Tiger was devouring the Nike shoes from China factory by 2004.

And China, the factory of the world, was planning the next lap with Andrew of Fortescue after having established a monopoly of steel products.

6:   *Rice, crude oil & iron ore*

There is something common about rice, crude oil & iron ore.

They all come out of the ground or soil.

We may think that rice is easy to grow & that crude oil and iron ore are harder to produce.

But in reality, the very opposite is true.

We think rice is easy to grow as we can see rice sprouting from the fields on its own. You only need some labour to till the soil, we perceive.

On the other hand, high tech engineers need to produce crude oil & iron ore, we perceive.

They need massive capital & technology, we perceive.

Unlike the rice fields, we cannot see the oil fields & iron ore mines.

If you are within 2000 kms of Saudi Arabia & if you push a small 2" pipe into the soil, oil or gas may sprout out.

If you are right in Saudi Arabia, you may need to push in a larger 8" pipe in the ground with a small drilling machine to get crude oil.

But once you hit the oil reservoir, it will gush out & it is difficult to stop the crude oil from gushing out.

If you want more oil faster, you insert a larger pipe in the ground.

So unlike rice for which you have to work hard for months, oil gushes out of the ground with little effort.

The crude oil gushes out of the ground.

What about iron ore?

When we hear of an iron ore mine, we may think of tunnels and shafts deep down. But that is a coal mine.

The iron ore mine is often an open pit. You scoop it up with a bucket. If you want to grab it faster, you may use a machine to scoop it up.

In short, crude oil & iron ore are extracted easier than growing rice in the paddy fields.

So that would explain the lack of any X factor for the iron ore when we deal with the cost of production.

There is another significant difference of the impact of prices of crude oil & iron ore.

It is true that crude oil price affects energy cost and therefore affects everybody. But billions of people may not be using oil energy. They may be using fire wood.

The price of crude oil substantially affects the petrol prices or gasoline prices. So we can say that crude oil prices affect the rich than they affect the poor.

Or at least we can say that they affect richer people more & they affect poorer people less.

So we can say that when Saudi Arabia sells crude oil at false prices, the money comes out of richer pockets rather than poorer pockets.

But that is not the same for iron ore prices. Iron ore prices affect the cost of your pots & pans and your sickles. It affects your house structure & your fence. It affects all your stainless steel spoons & stainless steel ware.

So iron ore prices are affecting the people across the poor and rich spectrum. It creeps in almost everything in our daily lives without our conscious knowledge of it.

7: The cost of production Vs market prices

When Thai farmer produces rice at a cost of $1 a kg, he sells it at $1.15 only.

There are so many Thai farmers who want to sell it at that price.

So the cost of production is inherent in the supply and demand theory (more or less).

If Americans make Nike shoe at a cost of $50 a shoe & if the Chinese can make it for $10 a shoe, Americans will go to China to make them rather than they making them.

When one sells Palm Jumeira villa in Dubai at $8 million a villa, it may have been built for $1 million but the buyer may have bought it at $2 million or $6 million.

So when it comes to property prices, the cost of production factor is rather hazy.

But that is not the case of Sam's iron ore, God's soil.

Sam is bluffing that his cost of iron ore production is $20.70 in 2014 and that his cost is the lowest, unless he had increased the pay of the diggers hundred fold.

May be he had given out too much bonus to them to inflate the cost of production.

Vale, BHP & Rio (except Andrew of Fortescue) had been supplying iron ore at $10 a tonne until 2004 in very large quantities since 1984 & earlier.

So the true cost of production of iron ore should be hovering around $5 a tonne globally.

By 2005, the Asian Tiger had increased the demand. So their cost of production should decrease (and not increase).

All they do is to scoop up more of the iron ore from the same pit.

Believe it; it is only a pit.

It is not a mine like coal mine with shafts and the like deep down the earth.

So Sam was producing it at $5 or $6 a tonne in 2004 & Andrew of Fortescue (he is known as Twiggy in Australia) made a deal with Chinese to sell it at $28 a tonne in 2005.

Andrew had a new developing mine in Pilbarra in Western Australia & China had financed it with a A$2 billion loan package.

Sam of Rio Tinto & Jac of BHP did not offer the Chinese to supply iron ore at $17 or $20 a tonne in 2005 when Andrew was aiming for $28 a tonne.

Instead they embraced the new colleague Andrew & joined in the Shanghai party.

That is the story of the first high jump in iron ore price; a jump from $16 a tonne in December, 2004 to $28 a tonne in January, 2005.

Year by year, the party became wilder and wilder.

Sam, Jac & Andrew agreed with the Chinese to supply iron ore at $187.18 a tonne on a day in February, 2011.

That was the highest price recorded for iron ore ever.

It will be interesting to know how Sam can justify selling a tonne of iron ore at a price of $187.18 a tonne when he can produce it at $20.70 a tonne by his own claim knowing that it was the Thai farmer paying for that extra profit.

Even more importantly, it will be interesting to know if he complied with the Trade Practices Act of Australia.

It spells out that Australians cannot engage in "unconscionable conduct" in trading in or out of Australia.

Does Sam think it is conscionable to sell iron ore at $187 a tonne in any year; 2009 or 2010 or 2011 or 2012 or 2013 or 2014?

Sam, Jac & Andrew don't care for the Thai farmers.

They care for the Asian Tiger and the Asian demand.

This shows the relationship between the market prices, supply and demand & the cost of production in the real world.

Without the understanding of the larger world or perhaps even the Nobel laureates, this relationship affects the entire world, its well being & more importantly the equality in our world.

Billions of poor people have been forced to pay for Sam's extra profit of extra ordinary proportion made in the false name of Asian Tiger.

They were forced to believe that Karl Marx theory was wrong & that the free market economy would resolve the problems.

We should urge the Nobel laureates to make a better formula of the relationship between the market prices & cost of production if they care for the Thai farmers.

The Shanghai party of Sam, Jac & Andrew of Australia has now caused a real problem for Bill Gates in USA.

We can only hope that the great Bill did not sell his software at $10 a piece when his true cost was only $1 a piece.

Perhaps software had innovation & patents involved as opposed to digging up God's soil of God's land.

Without Bill's internet, we might not have figured out the Shanghai party.

Only with Bill's internet, we could figure this out that Sam sold iron ore at $187.18 a tonne in year 2011 while he claimed its cash cost was only $20.70 a tonne.

Did Sam, Jac & Andrew from Australia outpace Bernie Madoff?

8: *The Asian tiger*

The Asian Tiger is all about numbers.

A price rise of $0.10 for a cup of tea results in an extra income of $500 million for tea makers assuming that the world consumes 5 billion cups of tea every day.

An unnoticeable price rise of $0.10 a cup of tea amounts to $500 million extra income a day.

We should repeat it: **$500 million extra income a day.**

By 2004, the available people in the world with purchasing power had increased considerably.

This was the Asian tiger.

This Asian tiger was the meat for China & Australia.

Whatever iron ore China produced or imported, it was all used to make steel.

That steel was used to make cars, pipes & sickles.

So China would make a profit on top of that cost of raw material.

If the cost of iron ore component of a pipe is $100, china would sell it at $115 or more.

So whatever China pays for iron ore, China would make a profit on top of the cost.

If China used $1 billion worth of iron ore for steel production, it will bring back $1.15 billion for China.

In 2005, the world demand for iron ore was 1,530 million tonnes. China produced 310 million tonnes. China imported 500 million tonnes from Australia & Brazil

In 2011, the world demand for iron ore was 2,940 million tonnes. China produced 1,380 million tonnes. China imported 900 million tonnes from Australia & Brazil

A price increase of $12 a tonne for iron ore in 2005 would have placed at least $1 billion **extra cash** with China that year.

A price increase of $100 a tonne for iron ore in 2011 would have placed at least $228 billion **extra cash** with China that year.

That **extra profit** does not count the extra profit China makes on China's own iron ore production.

One can calculate easily what **extra profit** China may make, if iron ore is sold at $187.12 a tonne, when it is produced at a cost of $5 a tonne.

So it is the number of buyers or the quantities bought that add up to the final profit.

It was the number factor that eventually failed the Dubai property market.

The buyers were rich Arabs; rich Asians; Rich English & Rich East Europeans.

They must add up to close to a few thousands or even more.

They were able to collude to increase the prices when the ground was fertile until 2008.

But the effect of the Global Financial Crisis was too much to hold them all together in 2008.

But the Shanghai party was not the same.

There were only five people in the party. And none of the five would lose if prices climbed. Instead they would make **extra profit**.

They were Sam, Jac, Andrew, a Brazilain & China.

We can figure out the name of the Brazilian. But it is hard to pin point the Chinese. So we must call him China

Anyway, it is not the name that concerns us but the numbers.

When they held parties in Shanghai to make the rules of iron ore prices & when they held parties to set the rules of market games of commodities with derivatives & options, the party was held by a few people.

The billions take it lying down.

We have no question to the game players.

Most of us do not even know about the parties at all.

United Nations have no question.

World Trade Organization has no question.

It is all about supply & demand, the partyers claim.

It is all about the Asian tiger, the partyers claim.

9:   The instant billionaire theory

If you lived before the computer age, you would have heard of Karl Marx. He is considered an evil man by many while many more adore him & his aspirations.

Chinese used to adore him, when they were underdogs. Chinese communists identify them as Marxists.

Karl Marx wanted equality in society.

Today, almost 90 % would agree that they prefer more equality than less equality at least in economic terms.

So why is Karl Marx considered an evil man by many?

We should assume that many do not like communism. Karl Marx is known to have developed the concepts of communism.

His main theory dealt with market economy for laymen (capital for economists).

He figured that inequality came from market inequalities.

In fact, incidentally IMF also said that market inequalities caused Global Financial Crisis in 2008.

The concept was that the "middle man" ran away with all the profits.

Farmers tilled the soil, produced rice at a cost of $1 a kilogram & sold it at $1.15 a kilogram. The middle man bought it from him and sold it in distant cities for $5 a kilogram.

So the rice farmer got a profit of 15% while the middle man made a profit of 500%.

So we have the same story of Thai rice farmers of to-day & Sam/Rio Tinto/Australia and China today.

Karl Marx solution was the purest but unfortunately the most naive.

He invented a simple theory. If we cut out the middle man and replace the evil middle man with a "clean" government, then we can sell things at reasonable prices to the farmers.

The "clean government" would employ all, produce all & sell all.

In fact, he did not say a "clean" government. He in his naivety & simplicity of heart assumed that rulers or government would be "clean".

Now everybody knows the story of Stalin to Khrushchev to poor Gorbachev and to Putin.

We should say "evolving Putin" as we never know where that would end. He understood that free market economy has better potential for Russia.

Anyway, there ended the story of the "evil" middle man.

And it gave rise to a start to an era we are yet to discover.

We can call this now only as "globalization".

When Karl Marx said free market was the problem, globalization assumes that free market is the solution.

Instead of restricting the middle man, we should give them freedom to operate & create.

The many middle men and the inevitable supply & demand dynamics would solve it.

That is the crux of the free market economy.

We heard it from Romney of course.

But we do hear even from Obama who is called a "socialist" and even a "communist".

Non believers of free market economy and God's chosen people of Israel are subject to instant termination in USA, the bastion of free market economy.

USA has single handedly proven beyond a reasonable doubt that free market economy (or freedom) breeds all good things and all good inventions.

Practically all innovations in all fields except spirituality come from USA.

Free market economy also breeds another innovative theory.

The Instant Billionaire theory

If you own a Rolex watch & if it has a value of $1 million, you are a millionaire. If the value if it climbs instantly to $1 billion, you become an Instant Billionaire.

There may be only one of the kinds of that Rolex watch and the X factor along with supply and demand factors are at play.

Free market players are capable to embrace that simple theory & adapt to others in the market economy.

If you own a land in Australia & if it has a value of $1 million, you are a millionaire.

Values of land are fixed by Valuer General in Australia.

If he certifies that your land suddenly somehow has a value of $1 billion, you become Instant Billionaire.

So that is the simple Instant Billionaire theory.

Even if you say that all the Chinese are snapping up all Australian land, the question is "where is the X factor" for Australian land.

There are only 20 million people In Australia which is almost as large as China with more than a billion people.

If you have a tonne of soil called iron ore in Australia & if it is worth $1 million, you are a millionaire.

If China agrees to pay $1 billion for it, then you become an instant billionaire.

If you have 5000 million tones of it under your soil & if China wants all of it at that price, Australia has $trillions & $trillions under the soil.

The ingenuity of Australian free market players should not be underestimated.

Karl Marx said that farmers are suffering because the middle men were selling sickles & cooking pots at double the price.

He was complaining that farmers were paying $2 a sickle instead of $1.15 a sickle.

Australians ensure that cost of making them in China is $10 and therefore the farmers in Thailand should buy them at $12 a piece.

Chinese are very happy too. If Chinese sell a sickle for $1.15 of cost $1, they make only $0.15 a sickle. If he sells it at $12 when the cost is $10, he makes $2 profit instead of $0.15 a sickle.

Instead of hiking the price directly, they hike the cost of production.

So we should study this market economy of today in finer details & produce some basic data so that Nobel Laureates can study them further.

They can report back to us and claim some more Nobels.

10: *The fertile ground*

Materialism comes first in China. Spirituality comes second or last. Or it is despised. It is not a secret in Communist China.

There is profit but there is no God.

By 2004, China could see the end of the tunnel of profit.

The business of steel was all in China. The hunger for steel was rising globally. China's iron ore production was rising rapidly.

China was a willing buyer for extra profit in iron ore business by 2004.

Australia was fighting & bribing Saddam concurrently in 2001.

So criminality for **extra profit** was fair game for Australian government by 2001.

St. George Bank and other banks had successfully implemented the Ponzi scheme using "Instant billionaire theory" in land sales by 2003.

Australia's dominance in iron ore production was obvious for Andrew, Sam & Jac in Australia.

Australia was a willing seller for extra profit in iron business by 2004.

The higher the iron ore price, the better for both.

And it was at the expense of all others.

The ground was fertile by the year 2004 for iron ore Ponzi Scheme.

11: The facts of the Irongate

Alan Greenspan is the established champion of free market economy since the 1980s.

If you read Alan Greenspan's interviews since the Global Financial Crisis, it becomes clear that he takes the blame for the crisis. If not him, it was the USA system that failed.

That is the universal understanding. USA caused it.

Free Market economy failed. So it should be USA.

Free Market economy only gave the impetus. The Global Financial Crisis was caused by outsiders. Alan Greenspan is still clueless on who actually caused it.

Free market manipulators are ingenious. They are from Harvard & Oxford.

They create a frenzy of quick profit on others and then make a profit for themselves from those who got in the frenzy.

There is no trail after the kill.

Dubai Property market

The best example is its perfect implementation in Dubai property market in 2000-2008.

Sheikh Mohd is the ruler in Dubai. He has a great reputation as a hard working & well meaning Sheikh. He and his sons have excelled in all kinds of sports including horse races & endurance cups.

Dubai is practically a desert land or was one prior to year 2000. It is now quite modern and green. That is the positive part that they can convert a desert into a resort.

But that alone does not justify its implementation.

By 2002, the property prices were going up & up in Dubai on the excuse that more people were coming to Dubai.

The price doubled and there were rumours of an impending price collapse & that the market price rise was unreal.

But the next day, Sheikh Mohd the ruler of Dubai opens the now famous "The Palm Jumeira".

And soon the news spread that Manchester United football team members were all buying a villa each in The Palm.

That was topped with the news that Beckham was buying one and was moving to Dubai.

So the first phase of the possible fallout was silenced with that blow.

There is no real way of knowing the statistics of property sales in Dubai. You have to depend on the general news like Beckham & the never ending snapping up the properties by the rich Arabs.

The house rents were doubling now and then. So we have to assume that Beckham & the rich Arabs were indeed snapping them.

By 2004, things were getting back to the rumour stage. Again we hear news of Sheikh Mohd cutting ribbons to more launches of mega projects. This was followed by more announcements of additional developments at the Palm & the launch of the now famous Atlantis.

Then comes Palm Jabel Ali & even the much larger Palm Deira.

You could already see the bridge that leads to Palm Deira and the dredging machines were visible from the Dubai shore lines.

(Palm Jabel Ali & Palm Deira had dredging machines visible for the last eight long years! They know how to keep the hope alive)

Then comes the news of Tiger Woods coming to Dubai & designing a Tiger Wood golf course as part of Dubailand.

Never ending new names of new property developments are being tossed around.

Finally it was all topped up with tallest building of the world, the now famous Burj Khaliffa.

So there was no way the rumour monger could get any room. Every time the rumour monger shows his head, the shock treatment was immediate.

It is important to understand the win win situation here.

Sheikh Mohd is turning the desert land for billions. The buyers were spreading more venom to the market.

Those who bought $1 million property in 2000 are sitting on $5-$8 million properties.

Those who bought $2 million property in 2002 are sitting on $5-$8 million properties.

Those who sold their $2 million properties in 2002 would have snapped up more in 2004-2005.

There are no losers here. The only losers are the house renters who are paying rents which have quadrupled.

But they are hoping and planning to jump on the band wagon from the side lines.

Unfortunately, the Global Financial Crisis of 2008 was insurmountable by additional launches.

But the players of Dubai Property game are of course lining up for the next round.

We can see enormous amount of unfinished multi storey buildings all around Dubai now while new billion dollar property developments are again launched in Dubai with the fanfare of Sheikh Mohd.

The Palm Jumeira villas are still being advertised for $8 million a villa & we are left to speculate on the real market situation.

The shock treatments paralyze your sense of reality. The rumour mongers have no room to wag his tongue any further as rents and prices were & are still booming.

The secrecy of data as to who are buying the properties and at what prices they are buying them does not help.

To be fair, we have nothing to prove or disprove the real truth of the Dubai property market except for these known facts, thanks to the secrecy.

We have to assume that Beckham did not move to Dubai due to other commitments elsewhere.

Iron ore market in Shanghai

The Australian iron ore price escalation in China is similar but there are some important differences.

There are only four large suppliers for iron ore to China effectively.

1) Vale of Brazil,
2) BHP of Australia
3) Rio Tinto of Australia
4) Fortescue of Australia (the new entrant in year 2004)

Vale, BHP & Rio are and were the major iron ore producers & suppliers to China from early days from 1970s.

They have been supplying iron ore to China at a price between $10 a tonne & $16 a tonne for more than twenty years until January, 2005.

We have seen that all players including China benefitted immensely from an escalation of iron ore price.

They together fixed the price if iron ore at $28 a tonne from January, 2005 for the entire year 2005.

That was a straight jump from the $16 a tonne price of the month earlier. So it was a 75 % jump by five colluders at the expense of the entire world.

The entire world had no say in that matter.

They had prepared the world markets by now with the news of insatiable hunger for iron and steel for the growing Asian market; The Asian Tiger.

So the 75% iron price jump marked the game of value inflation that triggered the collapse of the Lehman Brothers in September 2008 leading to the Global Financial Crisis.

The Fortescue factor

Fortescue is a company mainly owned & developed by a man named Andrew Forrest (famously known as Twiggy in Australia).

He is now one of the richest men in Australia. He is one of the richest only because of iron ore and the iron ore price climb from 2004 onwards.

Fortescue is valued in the Australian market in 2014 at about $20 billion with annual revenue of more than $5 billion in iron exports all to China.

In 2000, Fortescue was perhaps worth $20 million & Andrew Forrest probably owned $4 million of those shares at that time.

The $20 million asset had grown into $20 billion asset by 2014.

That explains his current wealth.

Andrew Forrest was negotiating iron ore prices along with the development of his new Pilbarra iron ore mine with Chinese from 2002-2004.

By 2004, Fortescue had iron ore contracts signed by China for exports starting some two years later in 2006.

Just before the rules of iron ore price change & the consequent 70% price jump in January, 2005, Fortescue made announcements to the Australian share markets (ASX).

a) Fortescue announced on 5 November, 2004 that China was to finance Fortescue iron ore project in Pilbara, West Australia with a loan of **$1.85 billion**

b) Fortescue announced on 24 November, 2004 that Fotescue had signed contracts to supply China with two million tonnes of iron ore annually **for 22 years** and that an advance of $20 million was paid to Fortecue by China.

Thereafter, the iron ore prices were annually "negotiated" at the expense of the world & world farmers as follows.

From 2004, iron ore prices in the so called "Shanghai iron ore market" all based in China recorded as follows:

1) Iron ore price Jumped from **$16.39** a tonne in December, 2004 to **$28.11** a tonne in January, 2005

2) Iron ore price Jumped from **$28.11** a tonne in December, 2005 to **$33.45** a tonne in January, 2006

3) Iron ore price Jumped from **$33.45** a tonne in December, 2006 to **$36.63** a tonne in January, 2007

4) Iron ore price Jumped from **$36.63** a tonne in December, 2007 to **$60.80** a tonne in January, 2008

By September, 2008, Lehman Brothers collapsed, most likely due to the price inflations including commodities and land.

But the players of the iron ore market understood that shock treatment had to continue but now at even greater pace.

So they changed the rule of the game now.

By early 2009, they established "Shanghai iron ore spot market" in Shanghai which would establish prices daily instead of annually.

The highest prices in "Shanghai iron ore spot market" paid by China on behalf of the world were the following:

- 2009- $105.25 a tonne
- 2010- $172.47 a tonne
- 2011- $187.18 a tonne
- 2012- $147.65 a tonne
- 2013- $154.64 a tonne

The proof of the pudding is in the eating.

The world has eaten the pudding of China.

It will be quite naïve for the world to say that there is no evidence that Australia & China under leaderships of Andrew Forest and Fortescue had manipulated the Shanghai iron ore market.

Instead we should say with utter confidence that there is no reason to doubt it.

There is no reason to doubt it, given the extent of price fixing as high as $187.18 a tonne when the cost of production per tonne was not more than $20.70 a tonne.

Dubai Property market Vs Shanghai iron ore spot market

It is important to appreciate that Dubai property market in Dubai could not sustain the momentum after the collapse of Lehman brothers in 2008 and the subsequent Global Financial Crisis.

It is still trying to stand up after the hard fall.

But that was not the case with the iron ore market in Shanghai in 2008 or 2009 or 2010.

They were able to continue with even more vigour to unleash the same concept of Beckham of Manchester United & the Tiger Woods snapping up the Jumeira Palm in Dubai all in the name of another Tiger; The Asian Tiger.

They dismantled the long established "annual price contract" method (a game of five party price fixing annually) to a "spot market" in Shanghai (a game of the same five party price fixing daily) since 2009.

The five players, all with an interest to inflate iron prices ore as high as feasible, are implying to the world that they can establish better market values if they sit down daily rather than annually.

They figured that 365 chances (one chance every day) of their ability to manipulate the prices were better than a single chance every year.

The price of iron ore had increased to $187.18 in year 2011 from $12.45 in year 2000.

The results of wild iron ore price increases can be seen in the Loot chapter.

The True demand & the future factor

We can see two unusually high jumps of iron ore prices in January, 2005 & again in January, 2008.

If anybody raised the price of a meal from $16.39 to $28.11 overnight, it will be all hell for the one who raised it.

That is what happened early morning on 1 January, 2005 in Shanghai.

But nobody winched.

Nobody knew it.

Again it happened early morning on 1 January, 2008 in Shanghai. The iron ore price jumped from $36.63 a tonne to $60.80 a tonne.

Again nobody winched.

And nobody knew it.

China is happy.

Only prosperity can result for them for that price rise.

Sam, Jac & Andrew with the Brazilian & the Chinese in the New Year party in Shanghai negotiating the next year price was claiming that demand was too much for them to handle for the iron ore, unless the price was high enough.

They cannot claim now that cost of production was a factor since Sam had let the cat out of the bag.

Demand is the common feature of these incidents. "That everything is sold out and the demand is too heavy to manage".

At the time when such a claim is made, we cannot determine the true situation as it is about the future; "next year the demand is going to be very high".

That is the very basis of the price increases negotiated. There is no claim that cost of production was going up.

Was the claim of undue demand iron ore for future years reasonable?

What you notice is the opposite.

A straight line growth of iron ore demand can be noted for all years from 2000 to 2013.

While the growth of the demand was nothing spectacular, the price increase was simply phenomenal and unprecedented.

It rose from $12.45 to $187.18 in year 2011

When they held parties in Shanghai to make the rules of iron ore prices & when they held parties to set the rules of market games of commodities with derivatives & options, the party was held by a few people.

To be precise, the party was held by five people; all with one interest of inflating the price as high as possible.

The billions take it lying down.

We have no question to the game players. Most of us do not even know about the parties at all.

Alan Greenspan has no question.

United Nations have no question.

World Trade Organization has no question.

It is all about supply & demand, the partyers claim.

12: *The highjack*

Karl Marx is the guru of Marxist China.

The current success of China is based on its ability to produce goods at the lowest cost on the global scene.

So that fulfilled one part of the vision of Karl Marx.

The other part of the vision was that if you make something at a cost of $1 a piece, you should sell it to the end user at only $1.15 a piece just as the way Thai rice farmers of today do.

Today, China produces millions of tonnes of iron ore at a cost much less than $10 a tonne.

They produce much more than they import from Australia & Brazil combined.

Karl Marx would have wanted China to sell it in the world market at a price less than $11.5 a tonne.

Karl Marx would have been furious if China tried to sell it at $20 after embracing his vision wholeheartedly.

He would have called the Chinese "bourgeois" or capitalists.

By selling iron ore at $187.18 a tonne in February, 2011 in collusion with Australians, China has high jacked Karl Marx & perhaps even Mao Zedong.

Perhaps Chinese Marxists have become capitalists in disguise.

The proof of the profit is in the making.

13:   The trail

All production figures are in **million** metric tonnes

Year	Iron ore in the world		Iron ore in Shanghai market		Iron Ore in Australia	Iron Ore in Brazil	Iron Ore in China
	World demand	% increase	Price in US$	% increase	Production	Production	Production
Until January, 2009, the iron ore prices were fixed annually for the next year							
2000	1,080		$12.45		168	195	224
2001	1,050	(2.7)	$12.99	4.3	180	212	220
2002	1,100	4.5	$12.68	(2.3)	183	212	231
2003	1,220	10.9	$13.82	9.0	190	215	240
2004	1,360	11.4	$16.39	18.5	231	255	310
2005	1,540	**13.3**	$28.11	**71.5**	262	280	420
2006	1,800	16.8	$33.45	5.34	275	318	580
2007	2,040	13.3	$36.63	9.5	289	355	707
2008	2,200	**7.8**	$60.80	**65.9**	342	390	770
From January, 2009, Shanghai spot market prices were fixed daily on the spot							
2009	2,220	**0.1**	$99.24	**63.2**	370	380	824
2010	2,590	**16.6**	$172.47	**73.8**	433	370	1,070
2011	2,940	13.5	$187.18	8.5	488	373	1,330
2012	3,000	2	$147.65	(21.3)	525	375	1,300
2013			$150.49	1.9			

(Derived from US Geological Survey & IMF data)

Notes for the above table

1) ## Price rise is huge since 2005 while increase in demand is modest.

2) It is important to note that the unusual price increases started after a new entrant in Shanghai. That was Andrew of Fortescue financed by China in 2004. Until his entry, price increase was modest every year.

3) Annual % increase in iron ore prices was less than the % increase of production of iron ore yearly until 2003. Thereafter, the prices started increasing wildly though the world demand for iron ore remained on a path of normal increase.

4) In year 2009, the year after Global Financial Crisis was triggered in September, 2008, the demand increased only 0.1%. But the spot price for iron ore increased 63%. This showed that prices were "fixed" & prices did not relate to the demand of the iron ore.

5) The world demand for iron ore worldwide would be equal to world production, as there was never a shortage for steel products worldwide anytime until 2014 since 2000. They were always available in all parts of the world in all forms of finished products; cars, pipes, wire, beams, bolts and the like.

14: The ransom

The hijack of Karl Marx by a well planned colluded deception by China & Australia by implementing the Instant Billionaire theory resulted in a ransom payment by the people of the world since 2004 annually.

We are still paying it daily due to the inflated prices of every Chinese manufactured item when most of the world believes that we are gaining by buying the Nike shoe at a bargain.

But we have paid the ransom without our conscious knowledge by buying the bolt & nut made of steel at $2 a piece rather than at $1 piece.

That is the power of this clever deception strategy. We did not see or feel the hijack or the ransom payment.

Instead we believe that we gained by the unseen ransom because the ransom was paid in the daylight.

It appeared to us as a bargain. Everything made in China is better & cheaper, we perceive.

The ransom payment is not limited to the escalation of market values of iron ore and land by engaging in Instant Billionaire theory starting early 2005.

Instead it resulted in general escalation of prices of all commodities.

It resulted in the Global Financial Crisis four year later in 2008.

The execution is perfect.

China executes it with Australia. Alan Greenspan & USA takes the responsibility for the hijack, rather proudly.

China & Australia walk away with the ransom.

The total ransom paid is huge, in hundreds of $trillions. It is quite difficult to quantify with the data we have in hand. That will be speculation rather than estimation.

But we can calculate by a good estimation the ransom payment due to the iron ore price escalation and compare it with crude oil ransom paid to the Saudis.

Iron ore ransom paid to the Chinese & Australian until year 2012 is **$787 billion**

Iron ore ransom paid to the Australian until year 2012 is **$227 billions**

This meant that every person in this world paid a ransom of about $150 to China & Australia on the account of the iron ore pricing alone since 2004 till 2012.

Crude oil ransom paid to the Saudi's until year 2012 is **$2.55 trillion** (not billion)

It is all in the Loot chapter.

This is only one of the many ways the money from the tiny pocket of the man in the street gets collected in the manipulators' large net.

And it creates the inequality; a select few who collect the ransom and all others who pay the ransom.

15:   The Loot

Year	Iron ore in the world	Iron ore in Shanghai market			Iron Ore in Australia	Ransom to Australia	Iron Ore in China	Ransom to China
	World demand or production	Price in US$	Reasonable Price in US$	Overpayment rate in US$	Production	$ millions	Production	$ millions
Until January, 2009, the iron ore prices were fixed annually for the next year								
2000	1,080	$12.45	12.45	0	168	0	224	0
2001	1,050	$12.99	12.99	0	180	0	220	0
2002	1,100	$12.68	12.68	0	183	0	231	0
2003	1,220	$13.82	13.82	0	190	0	240	0
2004	1,360	$16.39	16.39	0	231	0	310	0
2005	1,540	$28.11	20.00	8.11	262	2,124	420	3,406
2006	1,800	$33.45	24.00	9.45	275	2,598	580	5,481
2007	2,040	$36.63	29.00	7.63	289	2,205	707	5,394
2008	2,200	$60.80	30.00	30.80	342	10,533	770	23,716
From January, 2009, Shanghai spot market prices were fixed daily on the spot								
2009	2,220	$99.24	30.00	69.24	370	25,618	824	57,053
2010	2,590	$172.47	35.00	134.47	433	58,225	1070	143,882
2011	2,940	$179.63	38.00	141.63	488	69,115	1330	188,367
2012	3,000	$147.65	40.00	107.65	525	56,516	1300	139,945
2013		$150.49	40.00	110.49				
Total ransom paid in millions						226,934		561,850

The Loot Table   (Derived from US Geological Survey & IMF)

Note: As the highest spot price in any year is used here since 2009, the amounts stated since 2009 may be marginally overstated.

<u>Loot in crude oil pricing by Saudi Arabia</u>

Saudi Daily production	Saudi Annual production	2000-2013	Ransom per barrel ($)	Total **($)** **trillion**
10	3,650	51,100	50	2.555

Production of crude oil is shown in million barrels

Notes:

1) The above assumes that crude oil price should not have exceeded $40 a barrel as its cost of production is less than $10 a barrel of crude oil.
2) Supply and demand is not in the equation of the pricing.
3) The OPEC/Saudi, oil majors and the punters have only one interest; escalate the prices as high as possible.
4) The oil market (as well as many other markets like Shanghai Iron Ore Spot market) is not represented by the ultimate end users. Instead the sellers and the buyers have only one intention; increase the prices and make a profit in the transit trades.

16:   The Bonanza

The iron ore mines in China are all owned by the government. Or they are state backed.

China produced 1,300 million tonnes of iron ore in year 2011. Let us leave the additional 900 million tonnes of iron ore they imported and converted to steel & steel products.

They produced within China the 1,300 million tonne iron ore at a maximum cost of $5 a tonne in 2011.

So the total cost of production of the iron ore in 2011 was only $6.5 billion.

In year 2011, the iron ore traded at an average price of $130 a tonne.

It is quite speculative at what price the government owned mills would buy the iron ore from their mines when they were paying $130 a tonne to the Australians in year 2011.

Let us say that they bought it at $100 a tonne. So the mines sold the iron ore to the mills at $65 billion.

We have to pause and think a bit.

Mines owned by China sold iron ore and earned $65 billion and made $59 million profit in just one year in 2011.

Surely Chinese Premier knew this performance though he may now claim that he had no time to waste time on the dirt called "black gold".

But the point is that Chinese Premier knew about the 2011 bonanza of $59 billion profit from $6.5 billion cost.

The landlord knows when he makes bonanza of a grand harvest in his field. And he will give his foreman an extra dime that day.

In fact, Chinese Premier would have known the iron ore profit bonanza since year 2005 when it all started.

Now the mills owned by China converts the $65 billion iron ore into steel.

Let us assume that cost of making them into steel is $10 billion. So the mills have the steel at a cost of $75 billion.

Again it is rather speculative. But they will not sell it for less than $90 billion.

So now we have another $15 billion profit bonanza.

So the mills sell this to the pipe makers. For simplicity, let us say that they sold the whole steel to pipe makers.

The pipe makers' cost to make the steel bought for $90 billion into pipe is estimated at $20 billion. So the cost of production of steel pipes is $110 billion.

Let us say that they would sell it to the world at $130 billion.

The profit is $20 billion.

So China made a profit bonanza of $ 94 billion ($59 + $15 +$20=$94) out of the $6.5 billion iron ore in year 2011 .

And that bonanza is just for the iron ore they produced within China in one year in 2011.

The bonanza calculated above excludes the profits made out of iron ore imported and profit made out of all other commodities.

The commodity prices followed the trend of the iron ore prices. So we should assume that China, Rio, BHP & the commodity majors played the same Shanghai game; **"pot bought on spot".**

IMF repeatedly warns that Australian properties are overvalued without specifics.

Interestingly, a close study of Australian property valuations may give some answers to the origins of the "Shanghai iron ore spot market" games played far away from Australia but in China.

17: The Landgate

By 2004, we had Watergate, Camillagate & Monicagate.

At that time, Western Australia aptly named its newly formed land authority **Landgate**.

At the very inception, they recognized it as a scam.

The land value inflation or issuing false Interim Valuation (equal to issuing false birth certificates) and issuing two Interim Valuations (two different birth certificates with different birth dates in each) was the standard procedure by 2002 in land valuations in Western Australia.

So the name given in 2004 **Landgate** correctly identified the conduct of land transactions in Western Australia.

By 2000, Australia had realized that Australia would remain "down under" forever unless the Instant Billionaire theory was implemented.

Australia is almost as large an area as China.

While China's population was above a billion, Australia's population was below 18 million in 1990.

Since land was in abundance, land was very cheap in those days.

The remote villages were scarcely populated & the land in those areas was dead cheap.

On the other hand, Queensland with Gold Coast & Sunshine Beach commanded some value.

By 2000, Queensland was transforming into a land of demand. But that was limited to the so called 'Gold Coast" of the Queensland only.

Western Australia realized that it was fertile ground for implementing

Instant Billionaire theory by year 2000.

Western Australia and St. George bank took the lead & the vehicle for

the implementation was **Landgate**.

18:   The vision

Today, most up market apartments in London are sold in the suites of luxury hotels in Hong Kong.

The expensive apartments are snapped up by rich buyers of Hong Kong allowing the London property prices to soar.

In 2001 to 2006, ocean front lots or land lots facing the ocean for single residential use in Gold Coast in Queensland Australia were sold at a price level of A$ 800,000 and above.

Those days many such lots were sold at property shows in the hotels of Hong Kong, Singapore & Dubai.

Similar lots in unknown & remote parts of Australia were also sold.

Some of them were superior to the Gold Coast land in natural beauty though they were in remote wilderness with a few fishermen living there.

Somebody living in Dubai may think that buying a good ocean front lot in such wilderness at a price at A$ 300,000 may be a bargain in 2002 in the resource rich Australia, irrespective of the remoteness or wilderness.

One such lot in panoramic **Southport of Port Bouvard** at Dawesville village in Western Australia was sold at a price of A$ 300,000 in Dubai in 2002.

The true value of that lot in 2002 was less than A$40,000 when it was sold in Dubai for A$300,000.

Another lot in even more picturesque **KalbarriVision** in Kalbarri fishing village in Western Australia was sold at A$ 567,500 in Dubai in 2006.

The true value of that lot in 2006 was less than A$10,000 when it was sold in Dubai for A$567,000.

One can easily see that scale of deception had peaked by 2006.

Both developments were in remote villages with only a few inhabitants nearby.

But both were bought at the back of an assurance that all lots in the developments were sold out due to very heavy demand. The claim was that people were snapping up the land lots as soon as they were released.

Both these developments were financed by property financiers called **St. George Bank**.

What buyers did not know when buying them was that both developers were engaging **the Instant Billionaire** theory; the vision of the Australian outbackers.

19:   The facts of the Landgate

Southport Estate at Port Bouvard in Dawesville village

The entire land of this development was valued at A$1.15 million in year 2000.

Approximately 50 % of that land was sold by 2007 for about A$150 million

So the land value in this remote village had increased 300 fold in just seven years.

KalbarriVision

The entire land for the entire development was valued at A$1.1 million in year 2006.

Approximately 5 % of that land was sold by 2006 for about A$30 million

So the land value in this remote village had increased 600 fold in the same year.

We should repeat that: **the value increased 600 fold the same year**.

Both are outstanding marketing feats at the first glance.

Both of them happened only because Landgate/ Valuer General had issued false birth certificates for the newly created land in both the developments.

The developer cannot sell land valued at A$1.1 million at $30 million unless Valuer General certifies that the land was worth A$30 million.

So without the false birth certificates, these outstanding marketing feats in the Australian farmland are not possible or feasible.

Banks will not offer loan of A$30 million for land worth A$1.1 million.

But they will give that loan if a certified land valuer certifies that the land was worth A$30 million.

Surely they will do so if Valuer General certifies it.

So Landgate is all about issuing false birth certificates.

Duplicate birth certificates with two different birth dates (land values) are issued to the mother only (the developers).

And the mother (the developers) does not have to show them to anybody ever. They remain secret unless one does a research.

The provisions under s24 of Valuation of Land Act 1978 stated that land value shall not be inflated when subdividing a larger land parcel.

This made perfect sense.

If we are dealing with birth certificates, we know that duplicate birth certificates showing that baby was 10 years old in one & 20 years old in another at the time of birth are false.

If we are dealing with land values, we know that developer cannot pay lad tax against a land value of A$ 1.1 million & at another value of A$30 million the same year for the same land. These are the facts.

a) Valuer General had issued heavily false land valuation for the lots on 1 December, 2002 when the lots were subdivided & created in Southport Port Bouvard. He certified the lot # 11 Sanctuary Cct bought at Southport with a value of A$ 250,000 on that day when its true value was only A$ 37,000 or lower.

b) Valuer General had issued heavily false land valuation for the lots on 1 September, 2006 when the lots were subdivided & created at KalbarriVision. He certified the lot #124 Lawrencia

Loop bought at KalbarriVision with a value of A$ 570,000 on that day when its true value was only A$ 8,000 or lower.

c) Selling land above 10% to 15% above true market value in Australia is illegal. The above sale prices were made legal by the false valuation of Valuer General.

d) In other words, those two sales were falsely made legal by issuing false "birth certificates".

e) If Valuer General certified the true value of A$ 38,000 for the Southport Port Bouvard lot #11 at Sanctuary Cct in 2002, the sale of that lot at A$300,000 would have been heavily illegal.

f) If Valuer General certified the true value of A$ 8,000 for the KalbarriVision lot # 124 Lawrencia Loop in 2006, the sale of that lot at A$567,500 would have been heavily illegal.

g) When the developer claimed that all lots were sold out at Southport, only 8 lots out of 93 lots created were in fact sold in 2002.

h) When the developer claimed that all lots were sold out at KalbarriVision, only 88 lots out of 182 lots created were in fact sold in 2006. It is very likely that many of the 88 lots sold were given away to the cronies.

i) **St.George Bank** knew the deceptions of the developers & the issue of the false birth certificates (false valuations) by Valuer General.

j) They knew the deceptions because they were holding mortgages on the land being subdivided at Southport and KalbarriVision.

All these incredible facts of deception by an elected Australian government (not just individual officers) would not have been known or exposed ever except for one fatal error of Valuer General.

20:   The confession

Graham Jeffrey is the Acting Valuer General of Western Australia since 2005.

He is responsible for all land valuations in Western Australia.

He operates from offices called "**Landgate**" which deals with all land and property matters in the state.

Graham Jeffrey issued three confession letters in 2010 & 2011.

His letters stated the following:

"I am the biggest cheater of all land valuers as I have continuously issued false Interim Valuations & false subsequent valuations exceeding 100 % above the true values of land. Issuing false Interim Valuation is equal to issuing false birth certificates. But I am not sorry as I did them under instructions".

Those letters did not state so in so many words.

But they stated so in spirit and implication of the facts stated in those letters & in this study.

Any land valuation out of 10% brackets (+/- 10%) of the true value is deceptive legally in Australia.

Decisions are issued to that effect by Australian courts & UK courts.

The facts taken from those letters and presented in the table below corroborates **the confessions**.

Date	Lot	Birth Cert #1	Birth Cert #2	Subsequent valuation	Amended valuation	**% of deception**
1/Sep/2006	Lot 124 Lawrencia Loop	370,000	570,000		270,000	**111 %**
1/Aug/2007	Lot 124 Lawrencia Loop			540,000	300,000	**80 %**
1/Aug/2008	Lot 124 Lawrencia Loop			500,000	280,000	**78 %**
1/Aug/2009	Lot 124 Lawrencia Loop			420,000	240,000	**75 %**

All his original valuations were highly deceptive.

The above conduct of false land valuation is typical of the entire development of the KalbarriVision.

After issuing two false birth certificates in 2006 on lot 124 Lawrencia loop at KalbarriVision, Valuer General continued to issue false valuation for three more years in 2007, 2008 & 2009 by his own confession.

The deception had become sustained.

False land value is stamped & sealed in the area.

Though value of the lot 124 was amended, values of all other adjacent lots remained high at original values. This means that lack of amendment does not mean that existing values are true or correct.

These amendments and **the confessions** came as slip on the part of Valuer General. It was not voluntary.

It was consequent of an earlier amendment letter dated 3 October, 2010 **(the first confession)** which amended the value of the lot from A$540,000 down to A$300,000.

If that slip **(fatal error)** was not made by Valuer General, all these facts were rather difficult to prove.

In other words, if Valuer General had taken a stand that all the original values were accurate, there was nothing we could prove any deception in land valuation with any certainty.

It is that act **(the fatal error)** made at that time without knowing the full consequent implication that triggered the subsequent amendments amounting to serious confession.

The great importance of these confession letters should not be missed.

Without the three confession letters, all the claims that the Australian property prices are not natural & not fair vanish.

If General says war is won, it is won. If General says it is lost, it is lost.

If Valuer General says that lot 124 Lawrencia Loop had a value of A$570,000 in 2006 and if he does not confess on it, then the value is indeed A$ 570,000.

We should also remember that the confession came due to a slip (fatal error) and not made in good faith.

So it meant that false valuation was practiced as a policy in Western Australia.

It also means that the fact that Valuer General did not confess in Southport Port Bouvard or other parts in Western Australia does not mean that values currently existing there are true.

It may mean that Valuer General learnt a lesson in 2010; "do not confess on land valuations".

In fact, that was the written policy of Valuer General.

The policy #4.105 dated 31 January, 2006 stated

"A valuation will not be retrospectively amended to any significant degree when that action has been caused by an oversight of the approving, valuing or rating authority."

So the slip made by Valuer General in 2010 and 2011 when he issued these confession letters was against the policy: NEVER ADMIT GUILT.

21: The fatal error & the last confession

Land valuation is a licensed profession in all Australia since 1978 or earlier. Only those with valid license may issue a valid land valuation.

All mortgages are backed up by such land valuation to ensure that transactions are done at valid market values.

Valuer General issues land valuation for all land for assessing land tax notices. He does that annually on 1 August every year for each and every land.

If new land is created by any subdivision of larger parcel of land, Valuer General issues a new land valuation for all lots so created on the day of creation.

In other words, Valuer General issues a birth certificate (called Interim Valuation) on the day any land is newly created.

The function of Valuer General is to record the market values of land.

Such value is derived from the land sales of the previous year.

His job is not to set the land values but only to record the true market values.

If instead, Valuer General falsifies land values somehow, that would amount to setting or inflating the land values instead of recording the land values.

If Valuer General issues false Interim Valuation at creation (equal to issuing false birth certificates), it will effectively be equal to setting land values instead of recording the land values.

In other words, if Valuer General issues false birth certificates to all new land created in the state, he is in a position to falsify land values in Western Australia.

If a valuer issues a land valuation out of the bracket of 10% (plus 10% or minus 10%) of the true value, it is legally considered deceptive and the valuer is liable for full damages caused.

This is well established fact in throughout Australia.

On 20 March 2012, Travis Coleman, a licensed land valuer was ordered to pay full damages by a Three Judge bench of the Federal Court of Australia based in Perth Western Australia because he had issued a valuation at $1.6 million for a house when its true value was only about A$1.2 million.

His valuation was 33.3 % above the true valuation & he was heavily punished.

So if Valuer General issues a land valuation at $570,000 for land lot and if the true value of that lot was only $270,000 instead of A$570,000 when he issued it, Valuer General ought to be liable for damages as he is not immune.

Such a valuation is 111% out of the true valuation & should be heavily punished.

Under the intense pressure by the buyer who pays land taxes, Valuer General issued an amended land valuation for lot 124 Lawrencia Loop in Kalbarri Vision on 4 March, 2011. That related to the original valuation of that lot as on 1 August, 2006 when the lot was originally bought & was newly created.

Amended valuation established that lot 124 Lawrencia Loop had a value of only $270,000 in 2006 when it was sold by the developer & St. George bank at $567,500 to the buyer in Dubai in 2006.

Valuer General too had originally certified that lot 124 Lawrencia Loop had a value of A$ 570,000.

So indirectly he admitted that originally he had valued this land lot at A$ 570,000 which was highly deceptive.

His original valuation was 111% above the now established "true value".

That fatal error & admission of guilt by Valuer General was not made voluntarily. Instead it was made out of sheer necessity at that time.

The earlier admissions rather carelessly have made the confession inevitable at that time in 2011.

After resisting to amend this value of year 2006 year after year, Valuer General had by a stroke of error of judgment at that time on 3 October, 2010 had amended the value of the lot of year 2007 from A$540,000 originally to A$ 300,000.

Value of land or a change in value of a land in 2007 legally did not impact the value of the land in 2006.

But logically it did.

Value of lot 124 in 2006 ought to be lower than the value of the same lot in 2007 as generally the land prices were assumed to have climbed from 2006 to 2007.

So it was inevitable that land value of land lot 124 Lawrencia Loop in 2006 should be less than A$300,000 by the earlier careless confession. It could not remain at a value higher than A$300,000.

It was Valuer General who had issued the highly deceptive original valuation of $570,000 for land lot 124 KalbarriVision on 1 August, 2006.

By issuing this false birth certificate at KalbarriVision in 2006, Valuer General had created a false level of property values in the large land development from its very inception.

How can the same culprit who issued the original false valuation certify the subsequent true valuation?

In other words, why should one trust that the amended value at $270,000 was not still heavily inflated?

Is the true value of this lot #124 Lawrencia loop only A$ 8,000 or A$ 270,000 in year 2006?

Did that original deceptive valuation at A$ 570,000 in 2006 enable **St. George Bank** and Godiniland, the developer to sell the land & finance the purchase at A$567,500 in Dubai?

Is Godiniland, the developers of KalbarriVision liable for this deceptive sale?

Is Valuer General liable for this deceptive sale?

Is **St. George Bank** liable for this deceptive sale?

Did they jointly promote the Instant Billionaire theory in land sales in Western Australia?

That sale of lot 124 Lawrencia Loop was just one of the 254 lots newly created in the land estate in 2006.

By issuing false birth certificates to all those rural lots, the total value of the 254 lots rose to A$ 30 million from a mere A$ 1.1 million overnight.

22:   *The Scandal*

It is well established in Australian courts that a pleading should not contain scandalous claims.

There is no clear definition on what may be scandalous.

If Valuer General falsified land values by falsely issuing birth certificates, it can lead to scandal.

If Valuer General does so & if one makes that claim, then it may be interpreted as a scandalous claim.

But if the courts deny one's ability to make such a claim, the courts are extending immunity to Valuer General from bad conduct.

When one makes the claim, it may be dismissed as scandalous.

If one makes a claim that Australia falsified iron ore prices or land values, it can lead to a scandal.

This is the catch 22 for Australia.

The deception cannot be exposed as exposing it is illegal.

The Ponzi scheme in iron ore and land sales is well thought about & is ingenious or devious.

Even the defense to the Ponzi scheme is also ingenious or devious.

If the Ponzi scheme is executed by the government, it leads to a scandal.

And the scandalous claim is dismissed.

The Australian Courts can find that excuse in order not to hear a case on such a Ponzi scheme.

This is exactly what happened in DR 162 of 2011 in State Administrative Tribunal in Perth.

This is exactly what happened in NSD 700 of 2012 in Federal Courts of Australia.

One cannot plead that Australian government cheated thereby giving immunity for the Australian government from cheating.

23:   The Genesis

{The facts now available to us now strongly indicate the possibility that somebody or some group in St. George Bank in Australia devised the "Instant billionaire theory" and applied it in many property developments in rural/outback Australia from year 2002.

Those facts are limited to & related to two large ocean front developments entirely financed by St. George Bank in rural setting away from the cities.

Those facts are limited as the research done so far covered only those two property developments.

Both these developments are based in extremely beautiful beach settings.

But they are both located where there is no large population base.

If the land and ocean around an area of radius 5 km of the estates can be cut and placed in prime areas in Florida or California, they could be very lucrative. But the locations where they are now without a solid population base lack true demand for residential land.

That serious shortcoming was overcome by the classic falsification that "all land lots were sold on release".

These facts are detailed with documentary evidences in another book titled "Australia hijacks the world".

This chapter is only a brief of those undeniable facts. Those facts are that

- *there was a written confession by Valuer General of land value falsification at KalbarriVision*
- *there is an orchestrated scheme of land value falsification perpetuated by the government of Western Australia.*
- *The scheme was in place since 2002 or earlier.*
- *By 2005, the scheme was proven successful and the scale & the factor of land value falsifications in Western Australia had reached epic proportions.*
- *The collection of land taxes increase as land values increase.*

It is a win win scheme for all.

Land developers collect higher revenue.

Local shires collect more rates (taxes).

The government of Australia collects much more in land taxes.

Landgate collects more stamp duty for every land sale or land transfer.

The banks' lending scope increases.

The land assets held by the bank becomes more valuable.

The buyers can sell it next year at 20%-30% profit as land values keep increasing every year.

It is not unreasonable to believe that by year 2005, the scheme found its way to the property market in USA due to the operation of Australian banks in USA by 2005.

This may have resulted in the property bubble there developed between 2005-2008 culminating in the collapse of Lehman brothers & in the Global Financial Crisis.

So the roots of the Global Financial Crisis in 2008 were in Australia, we can presume.

More research on the activities of Australian banks in 2002-2005 in USA may help}

The deception of selling something at a false high price is not something new. The theory that "goose lays golden eggs" has been there for a very long time.

The deception that iron ore which costs less $10 a tonne may be sold for $20-40 a tonne was always there.

The deception that iron ore may be sold at $187.18 a tonne is something rather new.

The scale of value falsification is beyond belief & beyond logic.

At the same time, the falsification is good news for all in the property market.

It is good news for buyers and it is good news for sellers of the property.

The enabler of the new theory is now the shock therapy with "Beckham & Tiger Woods" impact.

That enabler is rather new or improvised.

The origin of these new inventions would lead us to determine the root cause and the origin of the Global Financial Crisis triggered in year 2008.

USA has time and again has taken the blame proudly & has claimed that Global Financial Crisis started with the property price escalations in USA.

The subprime mortgages of Fannie Mae & Freddie Mac were identified as the cause.

For laymen, it was caused by overpricing house values in a supposedly booming market in USA.

IMF has published a working paper called "What caused the Global Financial Crisis" in December, 2010.

For laymen, IMF says that it was caused by the financial imbalances.

We have seen that undue & perpetual inflation of iron ore prices in "Shanghai iron ore spot market" created substantial imbalances.

Almost one trillion dollar was misplaced in the bank accounts of iron ore magnates in China & Australia sucked away from millions of small accounts around the world causing financial imbalances.

The undue price inflation of iron ore started in January, 2005. So we should assume that commodity price escalations led by the iron ore price escalations have driven financial imbalances weighing heavily towards China & Australia.

Where did the property bubble originate & where did the Instant Billionaire theory in properties originate?

Did that originate in USA or was it exported to USA by some others?

Could it have originated in Australia?

We have seen earlier that Australia is capable of anything including bribing none other than Saddam Hussein while concurrently fighting Saddam Hussein.

We have seen that it was likely done at the behest of Australian government & Reserve Bank of Australia (RBA).

We have also seen the iron ore price manipulation, perhaps devised by Andrew Forrest of Fortescue.

We have seen that China benefitted more than anybody else globally by the iron ore price escalations while the world had an illusion that China being largest iron importers wanted the iron ore price to go down.

The close relationship of Chinese government & Australian Government is heavily published. It is no secret.

Prime Minister Kevin Rudd was elected due to his knowledge of Chinese language and his closeness with China.

Australian economic boom is all about China & China's thirst for Australian resources and Australian properties.

We cannot rule out that Andrew of Fortescue had invisible support from Glen Stevens of RBA & Peter Costello, the then Finance minister in 2004-2007, the boom times in the iron ore price falsifications.

There is nothing to rule out continued support of the present Australian government since iron ore prices and Australian property prices remain inflated perpetually without a solid demand to justify the level of their prices.

The Australian Property market

The Australian property was sold for peanuts in 1990s.

Australia has a total land area of 7,682,300 square kilometers. That is almost as big as China having 9,569,901 sq. km with a population exceeding 1.355 billion.

The population of Australia now in 2014 is at 22.5 million while it was only 18 million in 1990s.

So there is 374,000 sq. meters of land for every Australian while there is only 7,062 sq. meters for every Chinese.

Therefore if we are going by the supply and demand principles, the properties in Australia should be the cheapest in the world.

That was true in 1990 until early 2000. They were indeed cheap.

That situation changed entirely by 2002 & today Australian properties are one of the costliest in the world.

In the case of property prices in Australia, there can be no justification for undue price rise based on true demand. The low population does not warrant a price escalation since land is abundant & population is scarce & very low.

Therefore we can see the pattern between Shanghai iron ore spot market & Australian property market.

Price of Australian iron ore is jumping from $10 a tonne in 2000 to $187.12 a tonne by 2011 without any undue global demand.

Australian properties are said to be worth now $4 trillion. Land prices have gone up 1000 times in many areas in rural or semi rural areas.

Australian land value has increased from $1 billion in 1990 to $5 trillion in 2008, the peak of Australian property prices.

So that is the same Instant Millionaire theory at play at both markets with a common denominator: Australia.

Property developments by St. George Bank

St. George Bank is a hundred year old bank in Australia & is born out of property finance.

By 2010, St. George Bank was acquired by another Australian Bank, Westpac Banking.

From all indications, it was a rescue as property prices had declined after 2008. If you held a lot of land at inflated land values, you would need a rescuer when the prices dip. We have seen it with Fannie Mae & Freddie Mac in USA.

Do we have reasons to conclude that it was hushed up rescue package to hide the property price collapse in Australian rural outback?

Do we have reasons to conclude that the Instant Billionaire theory was invented in the mills of **St. George Bank** in Australia?

Do we have reasons to conclude that by 2004, Westpac Banking & National Australian Bank (NAB) have adopted Instant Billionaire theory learnt from St. George Bank?

Do we have reasons to conclude that Fannie Mae & Freddie Mac were engaging in property value inflations learnt from Westpac Banking & National Australian Bank (NAB) operating in USA in 2002-2008 & even now?

By end 2003, **St.George Bank** had successfully implemented a large property development project based entirely on Instant Millionaire Theory.

Southport land development in Dawesville by Port Bouvard

St. George Bank was the sole financiers of Port Bouvard Ltd, a public listed company under ASX, who developed and sold Southport estate in Dawesville village in Western Australia.

Land parcel at Southport commanded a value of only A$ 1 million in 2000. But part of that land parcel was sold for more than A$ 200 million by 2007. It is an outstanding sale feat if it was achieved legally.

The Southport estate was developed in six stages. The land lots in the first stage 1 were sold from 2001 to 2003. It consisted of 93 single residential lots along with a larger lot.

The large land parcel that was subdivided into 93 lots had a value of only A$ 1.6 million on 1 August, 2002 as determined by Valuer General of Western Australia.

On 1 Dec, 2002, this parcel was officially divided into the said 93 lots.

As per the provisions of s24 of VLA 1978, the law for land valuations, the total value of those 93 lots as on the same day, 1 August, 2002 (the standard date for valuation) should remain only $1.6 million.

On that day, instead assigning values totaling $1.6 million, the values assigned for the 93 lots totaled more than A $18 million.

So the value was inflated from S$1.6 million to $18 million (11 times the true value) by Valuer General for that land parcel.

What this means is that every one of the 93 lots earmarked for sale to the public was issued with a false birth certificate or inflated land valuation.

Each of the value was inflated 11 times as noted above. The scale of value falsification was 11 in 2002-2003.

It can be noticed that this scale of undue inflation had gone up to 30 in KalbarriVision by 2005-2006 from a scale of 11 in 2002.

An individual buyer of one of those land lots is not concerned or knowledgeable about the subdivision matters.

Nobody except Valuer General & Port Bouvard Ltd knew about this value inflation of 2002-2006 orchestrated against the statutes.

In fact that implementation of the Instant Billionaire theory could not be understood by anybody until years later.

Even years later, it is near impossible to know the deception due to the prevailing land valuation system in Western Australia.

Generally, it would remain a secret between the Valuer General (Western Australian government) & the developers forever.

But in this case, it did not remain secret by sheer coincidence of further developments climaxed by **the last confession** by the Valuer General dated 4 March, 2011.

KalbarriVision- A Vision to deceive

St. George Bank was also the sole financiers of Godiniland, a Chinese family business, who developed and sold KalbarriVision in Kalbarri fishing village in Western Australia.

Kalbarri is a tourist paradise with heavenly beaches with excellent surfing conditions.

But its population was a stagnant 1400 people from 2000 until 2014.

St. George Bank financed the purchase a large land parcel of rural land with an area of 12 million sq. meters at a meager cost of A$341,675 in October, 2003.

The area was large enough for 20,000 residential lots where only 1400 people lived.

A residential lot with an area of 908 sq. m created out of that land large land parcel costs only A$ 25.00 in proportional terms of the cost & area from the above data.

St. George Bank knew all these facts as they held the mortgage on the land they financed Godiniland to buy the large land parcel.

In May, 2006, **St. George Bank** financed a private buyer from Dubai to buy lot #124 Lawrencia Loop with an area of 908 sq. meters at a price of A$ 576,500. That was one of the 254 residential lots in the first phases of the development & newly created a few months back.

In conclusion, St. George Bank knowingly facilitated the sale of land lot 124 Lawrencia loop at A$567,500 when it's cost was only A$25.

The scale of deception is beyond belief, only if you know these facts.

But nobody knew these facts other than **St. George Bank**, Godiniland & Valuer General.

And they were the parties who facilitated the sale.

Valuer General facilitated the sale by overvaluing the small land lot at $570,000 on 1 August, 2006.

On 4 March, 2011, Valuer General confessed that its true value was only A$ 270,000 **(The confession)**

But that confession did not justify how a land bought at a cost of only A$ 25.00 in 2003 can be sold for A$567,500 in 2006.

That confession dated 4 March, 2011 came after the following occurrences which were all well known to him when confessing.

a) After buying the land parcel for only $341,765 in 2003, Godiniland sold approximately 300 land lots subdivided from the land parcel by 2008 under the brand name of KalbarriVision.

b) Those sales recorded revenue of approximately A$ 50 million.

c) In 2010, after making revenue of A$ 50 million generated out of a cost of A$ 341,675, Godiniland was placed in receivership by **St. George Bank**.

d) **St. George Bank** was bought by Westpac banking on 1 December, 2008.

A carefully crafted West Australian Land valuation deception

The provisions under s24 of Valuation of Land Act (VLA) 1978 were specifically intended to prevent value inflation when a large land parcel was divided into many residential lots.

Australia has good legal regime. Australia has licensed valuers to ensure proper valuation. There is a specific law not to inflate land values as noted above.

That is the creation of fertile ground for a deceptive scheme on property valuations.

One has no reason to suspect anything fishy.

It is within this background, the scheme of issuing false birth certificate operates.

The scheme is quite elaborate and ingenious.

It is ingenious because it is hard to crack it and was never cracked.

It is made so complex so that no one would believe it if you try to explain it in details.

So it is better to disclose it in simple terms in this disclosure.

The scheme in brief

If the value of a developers' land is inflated from a value of $1 million to $1 billion overnight, the developers may be hit with an equally inflated land tax bill against its inflated value of $1 billion. That may be enough to bankrupt them, unless the developers sell and collect cash before they ought to pay the land tax bill.

Therefore, while the undue value inflation helps the developers to sell land at inflated values & make them an "Instant Billionaires", the land tax bill may crush them in the process with a hefty tax bill.

They can easily pay the hefty bill if they had sold & collected the hefty profit.

But that is never easy.

Normally land in large development of over 100 lots is sold very slowly taking years though they falsely claim that "all land is sold on release".

So the scheme is specially formulated to overcome this "double edge sword" on the developers.

a) On the day of creation of new land lots, two false valuations are made on each lot instead of one value.
b) Both valuations are kept secret and only Valuer General knows about them for a year other than the developer. (this is equal to issuing two birth certificates for the same baby & keeping them both with him for a year)
c) Both values are heavily inflated with one of them overly inflated.
d) The not so inflated lower value is used to determine the rates (local tax/shire taxes).

e) The other heavily inflated value helps the developer to set the price for sale of land.

f) The higher value is also used to assess the land tax next year. If developer sells it fast, the developer escapes paying land tax as the new buyer has to pay it.

g) When the value inflation is overly high in a development (as was the case in Kalbarri Vision), the date of valuation is delayed so that land taxation on the developer is avoided for a year.

h) Or the land tax notice is simply not issued to the developer. Nobody knows about it.

When this scheme along with all the evidences & **the confession** was exposed within Australia with full evidence in 2011 & thereafter, **the reaction** of the banks, government, the tribunal & the courts along with the Australian legal community are evidences to establish that it was indeed an Australian government sponsored scheme.

24:   The reaction

This Instant Billionaire theory catapulted millionaire Australia of pre Global Financial Crisis into a billionaire Australia of post Global Financial Crisis.

It is not a theory practiced by isolated people or isolated groups in Australia.

Instead it is a silently sponsored theory of Australia.

It is the reaction of the Australian system (banks, the executive & the judiciary) that leads us to understand that Instant Millionaire theory is sponsored by Australia, capable of Wheatgate.

This is so because all of them avoided & skirted the central question of the matter

"Did Valuer General issue false valuation against the spirit & meaning of the provisions under S24 of VLA 1978?"

The question can be put more bluntly.

- Did Valuer General issue two false birth certificates for every land lot newly created?
- Did he inflate the land values in both certificates against the provisions under s24 of VLA 1978?

There is an additional reason to conclude that it is an Australian government sponsored scheme.

The confessions by Valuer General made it clear that he did issue false birth certificates.

He had corrected the birth date on one of them. It was A$570,000 originally in 2006.

In 2011, he corrected the birth date to be A$ 270,000 instead.

So it was proven without a doubt that the sale of this lot at $567,500 in 2006 was false.

Further it was sponsored by the Valuer General because of the issuance of the apparent false birth certificate.

These facts could not be disputed due to **the confessions**.

All of them intentionally avoided dealing with **the confessions** or they claimed that they could not see any confession in the confession letters when pressed.

And nobody had a sentence of defence on the matters.

The reaction of Valuer General

Valuer General had continued to record deceptive values on all lots in KalbarriVision from 2006 until 2009.

On 20 February, 2011, Valuer General admitted that valuations of 2007, 2008 & 2009 were all deceptive by amending them all by 50% approximately on lot 124 Lawrencia Loop. In other words, the original valuations were about 100 % inflated for three years.

That confession was followed by **the ultimate confession** dated 4 March, 2011.

That confession stated that the value of lot 124 Lawrencia Loop in 2006, when the land was created & bought was only A$ 270,000 whereas he had issued earlier its birth certificate at A$570,000.

The ultimate confession was different from the earlier

confessions dated 3 October, 2010 & 20 February, 2011 in two respects.

First & foremost, it admitted issuing a highly false birth certificate in 2006.

In addition, duplicate birth certificates were issued on all lots newly created in Western Australia known only to the benefitting developers.

Valuer General did not accept any of the claims when complained to him in 2011 about these deceptive valuations & duplicated birth certificates.

Instead, Valuer General gave a lot more deceptive answers to justify all of them.

But there was never a recorded attempt to justify **the confessions**. They were simply ignored.

Valuer General simply kept quiet or poured more deceptions on the issue of value inflation with respect to s24 of VLA 1978.

The reaction of president of Australian Property Institute in Perth

Australian Property Institute (API) trains & issues all licences for land & property valuers.

They also provide land valuation reports upon request.

In 2011, the question of s24 of VLA 1978 & the issue of duplicated birth certificates were referred to API president. But after accepting a fee for the services, he refunded it on the excuse that the questions should be referred to lawyers.

The implication was that the issue was one of law.

It was not true. It was one of valuation. It dealt with the issue of how a new lot should be valued.

If it was indeed a matter of law or question of law, then the tribunals and the courts should deal with them & interpret them.

It can be seen from the subsequent events that they too avoided dealing with this very important matter.

They avoided it by a series of illegal moves to avoid dealing with them.

The reaction of State Administrative Tribunal in Perth

When one complains about the decisions of Valuer General on land valuations, the complaint is referred to the State Administrative Tribunal (SAT).

The decision of SAT is final.

The supreme court of Western Australia may review matters concerning "questions of law". But other than that, decisions by SAT are final.

In May, 2011, the matter of deceptive valuation was referred to SAT under DR 162 of 2011.

Submissions ended only in May, 2012. The "question of law" regarding s24 of VLA 1978 was a key issue of complaint.

SAT was duty bound to decide the matter in 90 days.

Finally the decision by SAT was issued on 28 December, 2012 which was 4 ½ months late.

The decision was simple. SAT decided that the claim of valuation deception was scandalous & therefore a review by SAT was denied.

It is very questionable why SAT should take 8 months to decide that a claim of deception was scandalous.

Such a decision gave immunity to Valuer General from deception since it was scandalous to make such a claim in the first place.

So that was how SAT skirted this issue of false birth certificates in year 2012

The reaction of Western Australian Supreme Court in Perth

The SAT decision was appealed on 20 January, 2013 to the Western Australian Supreme Court on the bases that:

- It is not scandalous to make a "bad conduct" claim against Valuer General with solid evidences.
- The "question of law" was not considered but skirted by SAT

Supreme Court failed to accept it on 31 January, 2013. The letter by Supreme Court was very dubious with unsigned document and incomplete reply.

Finally on 9 April, 2013, Hon Chief Justice Wayne Martin responded stating that it would be a waste of money to appeal to the Supreme Court on the matters.

The reaction of Federal Court of Australia in Sydney

All the above matters considered by Valuer General & SAT related to false valuation of the land lots only.

The claim and responsibility for damages caused by the false sales by the developers & by the false financing by the banks remained.

The key deception occurred in year 2006. The cause of action accrued only when one discovered the deception. It was discovered only when Valuer General issued his **confessions** in 2010/2011.

The claim should be filed within 6 years from the day the cause of action accrued as per Australian Laws.

To be safe, a claim under NSD 700 of 2012 was filed in May, 2012 for damages for false land sales backed up by false loans backed up by false valuations.

The Respondents were **St. George Bank** and nine others including Valuer General, banks, developers, property agents who sold the land and other valuers.

Before a defence was filed, Federal Courts ordered security for costs at A$147,850 as applicants were based in Dubai.

That was a discrimination against Dubai residents.

Though **the confession** letters by Valuer General were evidences, the security for costs was ordered without and before Respondents filed any defense.

Further misdirection of Federal Court of Australia in Sydney

The Federal Court intentionally misdirected in the process of appeal of decision to order security for costs of A$147,850.

The order was not an order that could have been varied. It could only be appealed.

Instead, the court advised that it could be varied and then appealed after the process of varying.

The court failed to vary it.

Now the court changed its direction.

They now stated that it could not be appealed due to the failure of getting the order varied.

We can explain this in a simple way.

China Hijacks Karl Marx

First the court advises " Please turn right & then turn left".

When you turned right, the court closed the left turn.

The court trapped you.

25:   The Blindness

The key question was "Did Valuer General issue false birth certificates on new land lots?"

As the pressure to address the key question increased in Australia, the avoidance turned into blindness.

The key question was first posed to senior member Peter McNab of State Administrative Tribunal in Perth in 2011.

He finally ordered in 2012 that it was a scandalous question & therefore dismissed the question.

If you read a question and come to the conclusion that it was scandalous, you do not need much time to come to that conclusion.

But Tribunal senior member Peter McNab took 9 months to make that simple order while he was duty bound to order it in 3 months.

We could assume that he was seeking approval from Buckingham palace to issue a false order.

Meanwhile the same question under proceeding NSD 700 of 2012 was put to Hon. Justice Griffiths of Federal Courts of Australia at Sydney in 2012.

It was again put on appeal under proceeding NSD 617 of 2013 to Hon. Justice Edmonds in 2013.

They both skirted the question and ordered to provide A$147,480 security of costs to address the question.

They knew that such an exorbitant sum could not be raised. If raised, they could always find reason to dismiss it without answering the question.

The key question was once again put to Hon. Justice Buchanan in 2013 under proceeding NSD 726 of 2013.

He skirted the question by blurting out that it related to strata title properties.

That was a lie. It was clearly **not**.

It was again put on appeal under proceeding NSD 1808 of 2013 to Hon. Justice Jacobson in 2013.

It was Hon. Jacobson who made a direct statement on that question.

His statement was incredible. He stated that he could not see the question or the answer.

It was equal to raising a blood dripping knife in the Federal court of Australia and declaring that he could not see the blood on the knife.

In Australia, judges' orders may be questioned under "Judicial Review" in the same Federal Courts of Australia.

Now question was different.

"Did the court registrar & the four judges in Sydney issue false orders?"

It was pointless to put that question to Sydney judges as they were united not to see the blood on the knife

That question was put to Federal Courts in Perth in 2014.

The reaction of the Perth judge Gilmour was equally incredulous.

He ordered that the question must be served on the judges "personally".

Clearly that was not required per the Court Rules.

That was a trick by judge Gilmour to belatedly enable the four judges to seek orders to dismiss the question.

This question was also put to the Governor of Commonwealth of Australia in 2014.

The question posed was different.

"What is the cost and remedy of the West Australian land value falsification by skirting the question by the Federal Courts of Australia?"

On 2 April, 2014, Attorney General of Australia answered on behalf of the Governor.

He answered that these questions are to be put to The Hon James Allsop AO, the Chief Justice of the Federal Court of Australia.

The game of skirting the key question was now complete.

26:　The shock therapy

We have seen how Dubai successfully applied the shock therapy in Dubai property sales from 2000-2008.

The Australian Ponzi scheme in land prices is perfectly executed with the same shock therapy.

- Australia makes specific rules disallowing inflated land values of creation of land.
- Valuer General issues valuation for a lot at $570,000 instead of $8,000 on creation.

You are left in utter disbelief that you are forced to believe it.

- You get your composure and make a complaint to State Administrative Tribunal expecting quick relief
- Tribunal dismisses your claim as a scandal.

Once again you are left in utter belief.

- You expect Federal court to give you relief for obvious deception & confession.
- Federal court orders "security for costs" on the false reason of being a Dubai resident.

Of all places, only Australia has well written law on Racial Discrimination & the ruling discriminating Dubai residents leaves you in shock again.

- You claim that judges are deceptive
- Another judge asks you to serve the claim personally on the judges knowing that it is not possible in Australia.

The shock therapy on the world at "Shanghai iron ore spot market" is identical & is executed by Australia.

- By end 2008, the world is gripped with financial crisis with prices of everything collapsing.
- Iron ore price jumps every month ending in a peak at $ 187.18 a tonne in February, 2011 from a very low price of $16.39 a tonne in 2004.

When you least expect something, it happens in such a severity.

27:   The defiance

Now the news is getting louder and louder around Shanghai and Sydney.

"The iron ore market prices defy the demand".

The ingenuity comes into play again.

In 2004, the demand and the Asian Tiger made the prices to climb.

Now they are slipping down as grip is weak.

Now it is the lack of demand that makes the prices go up.

To put it in another way,

"I have no more strength to climb up; now it is my tiredness that makes me climb up even more".

It is quite unclear why the five market players have no grip to climb even further.

Perhaps, they have run out of place to hide the excess iron ore.

28:   The new game

The iron ore game went on from 2005 to 2014 in Shanghai iron ore spot market with five players.

The price climbed from $16 a tonne in 2004 to $187 a tonne in 2011 down to $108 a tonne in 2014.

The players are now searching for a new game to keep the price up for the "black gold".

If one goes to a pawn shop, one can get some money if you pawn your gold jewellery in exchange.

The gold is so valuable that you hide under your pillow or under the ground.

The news is trickling down from Shanghai of a new game.

Iron is being used as a pawn.

So the unwanted iron ore can be pawned & it will remain in the pawn shop in China.

So iron ore is in shortage as most of it is stored in the pawnshop.

We should remember that it was a deception that turned the iron ore into "black gold". They transformed the iron ore worth $16 a tonne in 2004 into the "black gold" worth $108 a tonne by 2014.

We should admit that Shanghai players are ingenious and they deserve every penny they steal! Or do they?

Perhaps we should check if there is room for another five in Bernie Madoff's cell.

29: *The prescription*

The nature opposes equality.

Inequality is the very basis of life.

But the entire modern history of mankind is marked by our search for equality & fairness.

We have established communist governments and democratic governments to achieve them.

We have established socialism & capitalism.

Communism failed with Brazhnev in the 1980s.

Free market and capitalism failed in 2008 with Global Financial Crisis.

Of course, there is a great resistance to accept the failure.

While seeking these ideologies, we have taken an indirect approach.

We assume that by electing or selecting a government, the government will bring about equality & fairness.

That is an indirect approach.

Instead we should seek a direct approach.

When we want to curtail bank robberies, we do not take an indirect approach.

We do not say that if we establish a police force, bank robberies are curtailed.

Instead we make bank robbery a crime and prescribe punishments for bank robberies.

IMF has determined that financial inequalities caused the failure of free market economy.

We should assume that if we eliminate or decrease financial inequalities, we may attain greater equality & fairness.

We have seen that **undue profit taking** caused the Global Financial Crisis.

China & Australia made undue profit and caused additional financial inequalities.

So the root cause of inequality is **undue profit taking**.

We should take a direct approach.

We should make **undue profit taking** illegal and subject to severe punishment.

30: The Naysayers

Free market champions like Alan Greenspan are right when they claim that market would correct itself.

But there is something very immoral about that concept.

Andrew of Fortescue caused it.

George Papandreou of Greece paid for the first tranche of correction.

Many more are still paying for the correction.

Andrew is still championing the Irongate on CNN.

It is important to understand why Andrew is still able to fly the flag of the Irongate on CNN.

Naysayers would convince us that it is useless to make laws to curb **undue profit making**.

Naysayers would convince you that all innovation comes out of profit making.

The naysayers have convinced the world that Irongate is the only way the market would work.

The market is uncontrollable, they claim.

But we have to understand that the market is uncontrollable because the people in control of the market are those who want to practice the Irongate.

They would ensure that a trading casino with the ability to make maximum risk is the only for supply & demand to work.

We should not allow Wall Street players dictate the price of our rice bowl.

Instead we should make undue profit making a serious crime

31:   *Rice & Rolex*

It is very easy to understand the difference between rice & Rolex.

We can live without Rolex. But we cannot live without rice.

Similarly, we can live without Rolex. But we cannot live without iron ore.

If we deeply analyze this subject very carefully, we will find the difference. We cannot live without those things which are taken directly out of the ground.

We unfortunately also cannot live without chicken & fish too. So we cannot live without those things which are found naturally on earth.

We cannot live without cars & computers. They are not naturally found on earth.

Some things have become indispensable. Many of those things fortunately are driven fairly by supply and demand dynamics.

Samsung would ensure that Motorolla's monopoly is broken.

Crude oil has OPEC & five oil majors.

Iron Ore has China & four majors.

This is where the cartel conduct creeps in. It creeps in only in the name of demand, when there are limited players in the game.

High demand normally means that shelf is empty.

Crude oil & iron ore are never ever in shortage as long as you pay the price of gold.

So it is important to have an exhaustive list of luxury goods & consumer goods.

We should not allow anyone to **make undue profit** on consumer goods.

They were given to us by nature & it belongs to all of us.

It may be argued (not without strong dispute) that the iron ore found in Australia does not exclusively belong to Australia.

But the fact that iron ore was gift of nature cannot be disputed.

Australia did not manufacture it. They did not cultivate it.

To dig it up, manipulate the price & **make undue profit** is highly immoral.

It should be made a criminal act.

32:   The Human Rights

One of the highlighted issues in Australia in the last several years has been the boats carrying illegal immigrants to Australia.

Illegal immigrants are seeking a new land of opportunity.

Australians are determined to stop them though there is more room in the house than they can occupy.

If **undue profit** was not made by some at the expense of the others over the ages, the world would not have been so unequal today.

There would have been much less boats going to Australia.

So it is the critical human right issue.

Do not allow Australia to make undue profit using God given resources by deception in "Shanghai iron ore spot market".

33:   *The last word*

We need democracy.

We need voting rights.

We need less corruption.

We need freedom & dignity.

We need level playing field for all.

We need honest & smart leaders.

We need jobs.

We need schools & education.

We need to be heard.

But they do not help if we allow ourselves to be robbed in the daylight day by day every day.

They shall not distract us from the basic issue.

It is our fundamental human right not to be cheated.

It is our fundamental right to trust our neighbor.

If China & Australia say that market value of iron ore is $108 a tonne, it must be reasonably so.

Making undue profit is a very serious crime.

34:   *The Revelation*

It was a fine evening. Stars were bright in the sky. There appeared to have many Suns and Moons that evening far up in the sky

There was a large gathering with a podium leading up on a large stage.

The stage was heavily decorated with incredible lights one has never seen before.

The stage had six decorated seats all good for emperors.

In the middle, there were two seats. They looked like a pair of twin seats placed together. It was good for a couple.

Music was in the air. People were in a great mood of expectation. They were all dressed in colorful dress.

Then the bell rang and all fell silent.

A person in golden robes walked down from the stage to the mid level. All could see him clearly.

He greeted all and said that he had three proclamations which will be approved by the council.

The council will appear as soon as he read out the proclamations.

Then he read out these proclamations.

1. Banking

   After careful evaluation of the matters, the following are approved for implementations.
   a) There will be only one currency hereafter.
   b) The banking is hereby disbanded.
   c) There will be one exchange for depositing money.
   d) There will be another exchange to loan money.

e) There will be another exchange to transfer money.
f) Those three exchanges cannot have a relation between them.
g) Those three exchanges are not allowed to engage in any form of trade other than the specified functions as above.

2. Insurance

a) Insurance is self destructive business. A committee is formed to see if there is a need to manage risks.
b) If there is need in some areas, they will identify them and make recommendations on how to manage risks.
c) Life insurance is prohibited hereafter.

3. Trading

a) Nobody is allowed to invest in speculating trades using borrowed money.
b) It is illegal to speculate further on speculating trades.
c) Future trade is prohibited.
a) It is illegal to make undue profit in consumer goods.
b) The book defining undue profit is ready for purchase.
c) The book defining luxury goods and consumer goods are ready for purchase.

After reading out the three proclamations, there was a bell. The bell kept ringing.

A young lady beautifully dressed came down. She did not walk down. She flew down from nowhere.

She looked like an angel with wings. She was able to suspend herself in front of the stage.

Then she announced for all to expect the council to arrive anytime & to be standing in respect.

Suddenly there was a flash of light on the stage. A figure appeared. The angel announced.

Please welcome Prophet Mohd.

All clapped and rejoiced.

Prophet Mohd moved to the front seat on the right.

Suddenly there was another flash of light on the stage. A figure appeared. The angel announced.

Please welcome Jesus Christ.

All clapped and rejoiced.

Jesus Christ moved to the front seat on the left.

Now there were angels flying all around in incredible beauty & colour.

Suddenly there was another flash of light on the stage. A figure appeared. The angel announced.

Please welcome Confucius.

All clapped and rejoiced.

Confucius moved to the front seat on the right behind prophet Mohd.

Suddenly there was another flash of light on the stage. A figure appeared. The angel announced.

Please welcome Buddha.

All clapped and rejoiced.

Buddha moved to the front seat on the left behind Jesus Christ.

Suddenly there was another two flashes of light on the stage.

Two figures appeared. One was beautiful young girl in colourful sari with golden necklace. The other was a young man also dressed fabulously.

The angel announced.

Please welcome Sita and Rama.

All clapped and rejoiced.

They moved to the twin seats at the very centre.

Somewhere in the crowd, a little girl asked "where are we, papa?"

The answer came swiftly.

We are in heaven, dear.

ABOUT THE AUTHOR

The author was asked to conduct detailed research in the land valuations in Western Australia in 2009 soon after the Global Financial Crisis.

In particular, there were unusual price falls in the two land estates under study. The study was to investigate why certain estates suffered unusual drop in market prices

This book is the result of the research done in the last five longs years on that subject.

That research led to the iron ore story.

The research led to that story because of the similarities in the two fields; that there was an organized & widespread attempt to manipulate market values in Australia, the only way to climb out from "down under" for Australia.

www.ingramcontent.com/pod-product-compliance
Lightning Source LLC
Chambersburg PA
CBHW051811170526
45167CB00005B/1973